HOW TO GROW AN EFFECTIVE MISSIONS PROGRAM IN YOUR CHURCH

Sherman Pemberton/Glen Elliott

 STANDARD PUBLISHING

Cincinnati, Ohio   18-03020

This workbook represents the contributions of many faithful servants whose lives are given to Christ's global cause of evangelization. So many have had a significant part in shaping us and in developing this workbook that it is not possible to list everyone here. We count it a privilege to serve with these faithful saints and humbly recognize their contributions in our lives and to this workbook. It is through cooperation and unity with each other that we can take the gospel to every nation, tribe, people, and language.

This workbook is dedicated to all the men and women who will use it as a tool to help their churches raise and send forth cross-cultural workers into the harvest field.

Scripture quotations are from the HOLY BIBLE: NEW INTERNATIONAL VERSION, Copyright © 1973, 1978, 1984 International Bible Society. Used by permission of Zondervan Bible Publishers.

ISBN 0-87403-760-3

How to Use This Workbook

THIS WORKBOOK IS intended for you in the local church who have an interest in evangelizing the world. It is designed as a step-by-step guide that will help you form a missions leadership group (if none currently exists) and equip that group to develop a long-range missions program for the local church.

This workbook is best used in a group. As your missions group works through each chapter, the Holy Spirit can create a vision for and ownership of the missions effort of your church. Each member of the group will also grow in his personal commitment to and involvement in world missions.

This process will be valuable for your missions committee or ministry team, but its value goes beyond the designated missions committee. This workbook outlines an excellent process for your church leaders (elders, church board, etc.) to participate in as well.

You may also want to seek the help of key missions leaders to oversee this project. Such a person could be a missionary on furlough, a denominational missions executive, a church staff person, or specialists like a regional director of Association of Church Missions Committees or a Task One Consultant (1-800-TASK-ONE). Task One consultants are trained to utilize this workbook in helping

Contents

✧

Here is an overview of the organization, process, and purpose of this workbook.

Your church can make a difference in the world. Just watch and see!

✧

churches establish an effective missions program.

You may want to use one or several of the ideas below in developing your own unique approach to using this workbook. Here are some possibilities:

- Schedule two retreats and cover half of the workbook during each retreat.

- Plan several weekend work days.
- Schedule one or more nights a month to cover a chapter.
- Assign work to be done ahead of time and discuss and summarize it at the group meetings.

You are about to embark on a journey of discovery and service that will change

your life and the life of your church. As you actively plan to make a difference in our lost and hurting world, which God loves, you can be sure that God's power will transform you in ways you cannot yet imagine. Begin this process of planning and discovery believing that God will do great things in and through your church. ◆

Chapter One

Antioch Revisited

NOW THOSE WHO *had been scattered in connection with the persecution with Stephen traveled as far as Phoenicia, Cyprus and Antioch, telling the message only to Jews. Some of them, however, men from Cyprus and Cyrene, went to Antioch and began to speak to Greeks also, telling them the good news about the Lord Jesus. The Lord's hand was with them, and a great number of people believed and turned to the Lord (Acts 11:19-21).*

I can hardly wait! Today is the day Paul and Barnabas arrive home from their missionary journey. It seems like forever since they left, and they've been halfway across the world. I well remember the day that we sent them off.

I was not one of those fortunate ones to see Jesus in the flesh, but I can testify that I am not who I was. I was one of the first non-Jewish converts. All my life I worshiped at the feet of images of stone and danced with priestesses to gain my salvation. Like so many I trusted wood and stone to heal my family and protect me from the principalities and powers. I feel as though I have been set free.

When the believers from the assembly here in Antioch talked to my friends and me about Jesus, one of the first things we wanted to know was why Jews would be interested in non-

Jews. They were, and are, a very separate people. Oh, we had heard about Jesus of Nazareth. We had received reports about His death at Jerusalem and His resurrection. But when we asked some of the local Jews about Him, they said He had nothing to do with Gentiles. The Messiah's followers were only another sect of Jews, and if we were not interested in converting to Judaism then we need not concern ourselves.

I have a lot better things to do with my life than to spend it avoiding certain food and people, so I was not interested. That is why those brothers—that is what I call them now—who came to talk to us were received so coldly.

What a surprise to find the first reports were not true! These brothers from Antioch said the Good News was for every person who would listen. Did we want to listen? Of course, we were always ready to listen to new ideas about the gods, but no one was willing to tell us about this God. How could a person hear the Good News unless someone would tell him?

We eagerly accepted Jesus as our Savior. I am still having trouble thinking of Him as my "Anointed One," but the important thing is that I am free from sin and death. Most of us wanted to tell someone else about our Lord. The only people we knew were non-Jews, so we told them our story. They wanted Jesus to be their Lord—and like us, they told their friends. Soon we heard we were being called "Christians." I wonder if that's because they can't call us either Jews or Greeks?

Only a few years ago the great persecutor Saul became the great evangelist Paul. Who could have believed such a change could come about? And what about Peter? Would you have ever believed one so—well, Jewish, could have gone into a Gentile's house? And then to learn that he actually helped those people secure their covenant with God. That led to a great cry from the Jewish sect, I can tell you.

But now it seems so natural to address a Jew as "Brother" or "Sister." Most people around here now think of us as one group, even though we have very different customs. You should see our weekly meals. They are a lesson in culinary diversity as we eat and share life together. Is it not a paradox that the very people in whose presence we were foreign are now the ones with whom we eat and even worship? So many things have been turned upside down!

I'm sure the Holy Spirit works to bind us together during our times of praise and prayer. In those times of worship we are open to His leading. I suppose that's why our leaders and teachers were so willing to hear what the Spirit had to say about Paul and Barnabas.

If I had not remembered my own conversion, I would not have been willing even to consider the Spirit's request at our last prayer meeting. As a Greek I had heard the Good News from a Jew and then went on to lead other Greeks to the Lord. Now I know there are many people in this world, and I am sure they would have a better life if they knew Jesus as I have come to know Him. But when the Spirit asked us to set apart Paul and Barnabas for ministry in other countries, I was skeptical.

After all, don't those people have their own gods? How could they possibly understand this Good News if they did not know about Jesus? And really, shouldn't we keep Paul and Barnabas here and send some of our people who are less well known? We need our best and most experienced leaders here.

Am I glad I have the practice of keeping my

mouth closed and my ears and mind open! What was I thinking? Just a short time ago I myself would have said, "I have my own gods and I am doing very well." Now I know that my dead gods were not going to save me. Now I understand I would not have escaped the power of those gods unless someone told me the truth. The Cretans and Cypriots are in the same situation as I was. I should have been able to reason that Jesus was talking about the Cretans and Cypriots as well as the Syrians when He told us to "disciple the nations."

The Cretans do not have even my limited background about the man named Jesus. But that's all the more reason to tell them. Who better to speak to those people than our two best leaders? Barnabas is a loving and sacrificial person. All people must want to be close to him and hear what he has to say. Paul has a powerful testimony about the changes in his life. He can gather a crowd by just speaking. I guess, when I think about it, they are the two best choices—not that we had much of a choice. The Spirit was rather directive.

It is just as well. Left on our own we might never have thought to send anyone to another country just to teach them about being followers of Jesus. Take me, for instance. I love to study the Word of God. I want to study the Word and maybe even become a theologian like brother Paul. So when I mentioned this desire to him I thought he would be excited. He is our greatest rabbi and a true theologian. But he fixed me with those penetrating eyes and said, "To be a theologian you must know Jesus. And when you know Jesus, you will do everything in your power to preach the good news to all people." I'll bet that's another reason the Spirit selected him to go to those pagan Cretans.

It hasn't been easy for Paul and Barnabas. John-Mark has already returned by himself, saying the work is just too hard. But I bet the harder we work, the harder the Spirit will work.

Oh—look at the sun! It's time for Paul and Barnabas to dock. I'm so excited! I wonder if they've changed. I'll bet they haven't had a good leg-of-lamb since they left!

From Antioch to Your Church

What you have read is a fictional account of a real situation. Real people left the relative comfort of Jerusalem for the Gentile world of Antioch. They found a willing world and moved to the unreached, receptive people in what appears to us to be a natural process. When we meet the Christians in Antioch we sometimes forget they began as Jews who accepted Jesus as Messiah and became a mixed group of Jews and non-Jews who were called "Christians." This group of believers set a new path for the church by inviting non-Jews to become followers of Jesus. Into this framework the Spirit came.

These "prophets and teachers" in the Antioch church the Holy Spirit spoke to were all Jewish Christians, but there the similarity ends. Barnabas was from Cyprus, Simon and Lycius were from Africa, Manaen came from Palestine, and Paul came from Asia Minor. Manaen was a member of the Jewish aristocracy and Paul was a rabbi. It is possible that Simon called Niger was Simon the Cyrene who helped carry the cross for Jesus. Barnabas was a representative of the mother church in Jerusalem and Saul was a renegade feared by the mother church in Jerusalem. We can be sure they had their differences, many of them. But what does the Spirit find them doing? They were together worshiping the Lord and fasting.

The Holy Spirit selected the church in Antioch to be His working group. The church was commissioned by the Holy Spirit, through the prophets and teachers, to send out Barnabas and Saul. The Spirit could have simply spoken privately to Paul and Barnabas, but He did not. He asked the whole church leadership at Antioch to set them apart. He uses individuals, but commissions them through His church.

The church is still God's chosen tool. Individuals carry out its work, and some individuals will stand out as its leaders. But the responsibility for accomplishing the will of God has always been placed squarely on the shoulders of the church. Unless the church commissions its workers, they are not sent. Missionaries and ministers may talk about going out to win the world, but they cannot go unless they have been sent by the church.

It is reasonable to assume that the Antioch believers had begun to form a group consciousness that would have made change difficult. The Spirit came along to uproot their plans with plans of His own. They had a fine group of prophets and leaders who seemed to be content working their local area. However, they did seem concerned about the Spirit's commission. They were open to the Spirit's leading. This openness made the Spirit available to them. They were the first to be called Christians —a new name had been promised to God's people for centuries (Isaiah 62:2). When they stepped out into a cross-cultural ministry, the Lord carried them deeper in that ministry.

Almost certainly the idea of witnessing to non-Jews was still a new and frightening concept to these people. Saul had probably told them of his own commission and how impossible it seemed when he first heard it. Now they could see the impossible becoming reality. They may have been praising the Lord that they were able to see the beginning of His promise to make all the nations blessed by His name. At the same time they must have been wondering where this outreach would stop— Jews talking and eating with Gentiles; slaves and masters sitting side by side. Surely the world was upside down.

Suddenly they realized they were in the presence of the Holy Spirit. A voice said, "Set apart for me Barnabas and Saul for the work to which I have called them." They sent those first missionaries knowing they were sending the best men they had. They supported them with prayer.

Those first Christians gave us positive examples in more than the evangelism department. They based their activities on their belief system, not the other way around. They learned their theology and stayed with it. They knew their own gifts and skills and stayed with them. Only Paul and Barnabas were selected to go to people in different cultures. The rest of the people were left to carry on local evangelism.

The Spirit was concerned that the men who were chosen stayed active in "the work to which they had been called." He has the same concern for Christ's church today.

Do you hear the Spirit's voice in your church? It's the voice that says, "You have begun a good work. You are ministering where you are. But there is more —don't stop now."

In this book we want to offer a strategy similar to that early church. We want to help you create an atmosphere in your church that allows for immediate and decisive response to

Don't Miss the Mandate

"Go into all the world and preach the good news to all creation."
—*Mark 16:15*

"This is what is written: The Christ will suffer and rise from the dead on the third day, and repentance and forgiveness of sins will be preached in his name to all nations, beginning in Jerusalem."
—*Luke 24:46, 47*

"As the Father has sent me, I am sending you."
—*John 20:21*

"But you will receive power when the Holy Spirit comes on you; and you will be my witnesses in Jerusalem, and in all Judea and Samaria, and to the ends of the earth."
—*Acts 1:8*

"All authority in heaven and on earth has been given to me. Therefore go and make disciples of all nations, baptizing them in the name of the Father and of the Son and of the Holy Spirit, and teaching them to obey everything I have commanded you."
—*Matthew 28:18-20*

✧

Just so His followers wouldn't miss this mandate, Jesus stated and restated it in the first five books of the New Testament!

✧

the Spirit's call. We want the body of Christ to once again live up to its name, as the believers in Antioch did. We pray that as you work through these pages you will come face-to-face with God's mission and your place in that mission. When an atmosphere of mission is present in the body of Christ the best leaders will reach out to the lost; the local body will witness across ethnic boun-daries, the total program of the church will have one task, and Task One will be global outreach.

Global Mission and the Local Response

The word "mission" comes from the Latin word *mitto*, which means, "to send or cause someone to go for some purpose to accomplish some goal." *Mitto* was used by the Latin translators for the Greek word *apostello*, which also means to send. In fact, we get our word "apostle" in the New Testament from this Greek word. An apostle is an officially "sent one" to carry an authoritative mes-sage. The root of mission, then, involves sending. But who is doing the sending? Who is being sent? Why are they being sent?

We agree that evangelism is not an option and that there is "no other name given under heaven by which we must be saved" than the name of Jesus. We can be certain people will not call on the name of Jesus unless they hear that name. Someone must go and tell the unsaved about the good news and someone must send them. "Everyone who calls on the name of the Lord will be saved. How, then, can they call on the one they have not believed in? And how can they believe in the one of whom they have not heard? And how can they hear without someone preaching to them? And how can they preach unless they are sent?" (Romans 10:13-15)

Paul is going back to the issue of mission. These apostles, or "sent ones" of the early church, understood that they were under orders from the Lord Jesus Christ to carry His message to the rest of the world. Jesus had provided atonement for all mankind, but that atonement would be ineffectual without its communication and acceptance by its hearers.

The mission of the church is to disciple *every* ethnic group, clan, and tribe of people in Jesus Christ. It is not enough to say we have preached the gospel. The mission is not complete until people swear alle-giance to Jesus and go out to make disciples in their own way. New disciples need to know how to reproduce themselves.

God's mission is to bring the world back into reconciliation with himself. The Christian's mission is to make disciples of all peoples. The local congregation must commit itself to carry out this mission. Dr. Mont W. Smith observed in his essay, *Missions and the New Covenant*, "It would be difficult for a Christian or a church to claim to be moral but have no immediate and helpful relationship to world mission." (Smith, 1987, p. 26).

We do well to target the world and continue to keep the whole globe in view at all times. We can be grateful to such authors as Patrick Johnstone, who in his book, *Operation World,* challenges us to pray for the entire world while working where we can. Nevertheless, we are forced to think in smaller chunks of the world when it comes to our own response to mission. No one church or agency can reach all three billion unreached and unchurched people. Therefore, we set our sights on smaller goals with appropriate strategies, and this practice we call "missions." If *mission* is to offer recon-ciliation to the world, *missions* is the sum of the specific strategies of local congregations to fulfill mission.

Missions is the product of mission. Missions is the local congregation's response to understanding and attempting to obey mission. In biblical terms there is very little difference between "missions" and evangelism. Evangelism, as used in the New Testament, assumes world evangelism, though in many churches it is defined as local evangelism. Missions assumes world evangelism across cultural barriers. We will continue to use the word "missions" in its cross-cultural sense, because as Dr. Peter Wagner points out in his book, *On the Crest of the Wave*, it is important to recognize the different requirements and gifts needed to minister cross-culturally.

Your missions program will involve members of your body, some who will be "goers" and some who will be "senders." Both the goer and the sender are fulfilling the church's mission, only in different ways. The senders are those who will prayerfully and financially support the goers, who will be making disciples among other cultures.

There is a special relationship between these two kinds of people. When the apostle Paul wrote from prison in Rome to the first congregation he had planted in Europe, he said, "In all my prayers for all of you, I always pray with joy because of your partnership in the gospel from the first day until now" (Philippians 1:4, 5). The Greek word for partnership is *koinonia,* and the word is translated many times as "fellowship." Paul felt that the congregation in Philippi shared in a significant way in his ministry.

Each of us, as Christians, must determine whether he is a goer or a sender. We may change our role from time to time, but we should not be in doubt when asked about our involvement in world mission. ◆

To help you determine whether you're a goer or a sender, some of the options open in each category are listed here. Look over the list to help you decide which you are and which you would like to be. These options might best be called responsibilities and, therefore, carry a weight you will want to seriously consider before adopting one or the other.

✧

Goers and Senders

Goer's Options:
- ❏ full-time missionary
- ❏ tentmaker
- ❏ support missionary
- ❏ short term (two years) missionary
- ❏ mission agency worker
- ❏ cross-cultural trainer/recruiter
- ❏ other options: _____

Sender's Options:
- ❏ prayer warrior
- ❏ commitment of money
- ❏ shepherd of missionary or missionary children
- ❏ host for international students
- ❏ writing for encouragement
- ❏ missions committee member
- ❏ recruiting in the church for missions
- ❏ other options: _____

Decision: Having taken stock of the needs of the world and my own gifts and present situation, I commit myself to be a (goer / sender). From this day on I will focus my energies on being the best goer or sender I can be, to best accomplish God's mission through the missions program of our church.

Signed _____

Chapter Two

Your Missions Planning Group

THE MISSIONS PLAN-ning group or missions committee has primary oversight of the missions program—including finances, education and recruitment, and sending, supporting, and shepherding missionaries. This group is likely to be the people now using this workbook to establish or strengthen the ongoing missions program of your church.

An example of the condition of missions commit-tees in evangelical churches can be seen in a study of one denomination. Only 75% of its congregations had a missions committee, and 57% of those committees did not require approval of the church's governing board. What this tells us is that 25% of those congregations have no committee and another 43% have committees with little influence within their churches.

If missions is to come alive in these churches there needs to be some serious rethinking. That thinking needs to begin with prayer and increased knowledge.

Depending on how your church functions, we suggest you either rethink your present missions committee or begin to form one. By working through this book with key people in your church, you can begin the process. If you already have a missions committee, you may want to use this book to strengthen your existing program by having

The Key Players

- ❑ Minister or pastor
- ❑ Support staff (associates, assistants, specialized staff, paid or volunteer)
- ❑ Leadership or primary governing body
- ❑ Missions committee chairperson
- ❑ Missions committee members
- ❑ Treasurer
- ❑ Youth sponsors and/or children's workers
- ❑ Adult teachers or group leaders
- ❑ Missionaries
- ❑ Former missionaries
- ❑ Missionary recruits and candidates
- ❑ Missions agency personnel
- ❑ Missions experts, consultants
- ❑ New members
- ❑ Veteran members
- ❑ Other

_____

Every successful venture has key players whose passions, gifts, and abilities each contribute to making something meaningful happen. Who are the key players in growing a missions-active church? Put a check beside the people you believe would be instrumental in growing your missions program.

the planning group make recommendations to the leadership as a result of what they find.

If you are shaking your head and thinking that change cannot happen, we want to assure you that it can and will. It is important, however, that you use existing lines of communication.

Qualifications

Three essential qualities should be considered in recruiting and selecting missions committee mem-

bers, as well as planning the ongoing training and equipping.

An effective missions committee person is first a disciple of Jesus who

- is personally obedient
- is committed to prayer
- studies and applies the Word of God
- is in significant fellowship
- is an active witness for Christ
- is involved in reproducing mature Christians

Discipleship is basic to significant leadership in world evangelism and can't be ignored. Look for people who want to grow as disciples—spiritually "hungry" people, not finished products. Appendix B lists some helpful resources that you can use to help grow mature disciples. An active, Bible-based, effective missions program depends on leaders who are committed to the lordship of Christ as they live out their commitment to make disciples of all nations.

Second, an effective and contributing missions committee member will be growing as a world Christian. A world Christian is a Christian who is committed to, interested in, and personally involved in

- God's priority that the world be evangelized
- world events that affect world evangelization
- strategies to reach the world's lost
- lifestyle changes that will help finish the task of world evangelism
- evangelizing the lost in and beyond their own culture
- eliminating both overt and covert forms of prejudice and ethnocentricism

Several good resources in Appendix B ("Missions Education") can deepen your understanding of what it means to be a world Christian. Missions committee members who are growing as world Christians bring with them their own motivation and contribute effectively in shaping your church's vision for missions.

Third, an effective missions committee member is gaining knowledge and insight as a "missiologist." Committee members do not need to be experts in world mission, but they do need to be gaining an understanding in at least four key areas:

- The condition and needs of the world:
  —the unreached peoples and people groups
  —urban growth
  —poverty
  —oppression
  —illiteracy
  —persecution

- The task and role of the church in world mission:
  —recruiting missionaries
  —preparing missionaries
  —sending missionaries
  —shepherding and supporting missionaries
  —educating and mobilizing the entire church
  —mobilizing other churches

- The current strategies and issues that relate to discipling the nations:
  —the role of national leadership
  —tentmakers
  —team ministry
  —cross-cultural considerations
  —the role of social involvement
  —international students
  —creative access to "closed" countries

- Your church's current missions goals, missionaries, policies, and programs:

Discipleship, growth as a world Christian, and basic missiological understanding provide content and direction for selecting missions committee members and for equipping and training members in formal and informal "on the job" training.

The missions committee is your key group of leaders whose character (who they are) will precede and create their contribution (what they do). Selection and training of these members may be a key goal for your church missions program, since you will never move your program beyond where your leaders are at in any given point in time.

Change Agents

Whenever change is introduced into a congregation there will be one or more people who will be expected to introduce it and advocate for it. These are your *innovators*. There will be another person or group who the congregation will look to for approval or disapproval of this change. These are your *endorsers*. Finally, there is a person or group of people who put the change into action. These are your *implementers*. Regardless what you may call them, these three types of people exist in every organization.

Look at the list of qualifications. Rate yourself on the scale to find your strengths and weaknesses. As a group, what are your strengths? What do you lack? What people in your congregation, because of either their personal qualities or their position, should you try to recruit for your core group? Do they exhibit growth in the areas listed in the Self-Evaluation?

Self Evaluation

Growth as a Christian
- personally obedient   1 ——————|——— 10
- committed to prayer   1 ——————|——— 10
- studies and applies the   1 ——————|——— 10
  Word of God
- in significant fellowship   1 ——————|——— 10
- an active witness for Christ 1 ——————|——— 10
- involved in reproducing   1 ——————|——— 10
  mature Christians

Commitment to or Knowledge of . . .
- God's priority that the   1 ——————|——— 10
  world be evangelized
- world events that affect   1 ——————|——— 10
  world evangelization
- strategies to reach the   1 ——————|——— 10
  world's lost
- lifestyle changes to help   1 ——————|——— 10
  world evangelism
- evangelizing the lost in   1 ——————|——— 10
  and beyond their own
  culture
- eliminating prejudice and   1 ——————|——— 10
  ethnocentricism

Growth in Knowledge of Missions
- the condition and needs of 1 ——————|——— 10
  the world
- the role of the church in   1 ——————|——— 10
  world mission
- the current strategies and   1 ——————|——— 10
  issues that relate to dis-
  cipling the nations
- your church's current mis-   1 ——————|——— 10
  sions goals, missionaries,
  policies, and programs

Innovators. Who is allowed to introduce change into the body? Is it one person or a group of people? Is the senior minister usually the one to bring in the new ideas, or is it someone else? Many people will come up with ideas for change, but what person or group is accepted in that role?

Endorsers. Who in your church endorses or approves of change? Who is the person or group to whom the congregation looks as if to ask, "Is this going to be OK?" When you find them, you have found the "change endorsers."

Implementers. Who puts the program into practice? In larger churches that is done according to a process and not one particular person or group. In smaller churches, often one person is the energetic planner. He or she is trusted by the rest of the body. The body knows that when the "implementer" prepares a program, it will succeed.

You are going to need to enlist the aid of these three people or groups if you are going to be successful in building a missions program. Do you know who these people are? When you discover them you have one more important question to ask. Are they open to cross-cultural ministry? Do they see beyond the walls of your church building? If the answer is yes, then they are ready to hear the words of the Spirit.

How to Motivate

Are you thinking you know who the change agents are but they don't seem moved to work for world evangelism?

Ask yourself, "What brought me to this point of ministry?" The process that led you to a world perspective may well be the same process that will lead others. However, not everyone is motivated in the same way.

✧

As a group, list the change agents in your congregation. Which ones would be essential to implementing a strong missions program? Which ones are open to the idea of cross-cultural ministry?

✧

Change Agents

Innovators

Endorsers

Implementers

Some people will read God's Word and accept it as their immediate source of motivation, while for others it is merely a source of knowledge. Is God's Word incomplete? Not at all. People are motivated in different ways. Just as one will respond to an idea they read, another will more quickly respond to personal testimony. Some people are motivated by ideas, others through relationships with people, others by a plan or process for getting things done, and still others by actual "hands on" operation.

If you are the type that is motivated by ideas and words, then the Great Commission will be motive enough for you. You are the type that values and follows directions. However, for many other people that is a command to be obeyed and not motivation to carry out that command. They must be motivated by other means.

Some of them will be motivated by meeting people who are working on the mission field. Maybe they could go to the field for a brief time and by seeing the injustice and experiencing the lostness of a particular group they would be ready to sign up for service. The U.S. Center for World Mission,

Wycliffe Bible Translators, and Good News Productions have some excellent videos and films about missionaries and the unreached people of the world. If you cannot take people to the mission field then you can bring the mission field to them by film or video.

Some will be motivated by seeing how the job can be done. They learn by observing a process. Show them a plan for accomplishing this goal of world evangelism and they will be prepared to do everything in their power to reach out. David Barrett and James W. Reapsome have documented over 700 such plans in a concise book, *Seven Hundred Plans to Evangelize the World: The Rise of a Global Evangelization Movement.* (Birmingham, Alabama: New Hope, 1988). Even though it is somewhat technical, Barrett and Reapsome have covered many of the main strategies for world evangelism and may have a plan some members of your church could become excited about. It could be a great motivational tool.

Another group will be motivated by actually doing something. These people will need to go to the inner city mission or to a foreign mission to help build

buildings or teach in churches or repair equipment. They don't get excited by ideas or process. They are motivated by doing. Many agencies are willing to help you organize such trips. *World Christian* magazine prints a list of such agencies every year, and most church mission agencies can recommend groups. For example, AMOR Ministries in San Diego conducts work trips to Mexico year round, and Lifeline Ministries conducts work trips to Haiti on the same basis.

The greatest motivator of all is the love of Jesus Christ. Paul writes, "For the love of Christ compels us" (2 Corinthians 5:14). The sure knowledge of our own lostness and Jesus' unlimited grace brings from deep inside a love that puts the fire of commitment in our hearts. Just as true love drives out fear, true love drives out guilt and duty as tools of motivation. As Jesus speaks to the church in Ephesus, so He also says to us: "I know your deeds, your hard work and your perseverance. I know that you cannot tolerate wicked men, that you have tested those who claim to be apostles but are not, and have found them false. You have persevered and have endured hardships for my name, and have not grown weary. Yet I hold this against you: You have forsaken your first love" (Revelation 2:2-4).

One Bible college student was on the brink of financial bankruptcy. Newly married and committed to mission work in Africa, he was one day away from losing his car and being asked to leave his apartment. When he was called to the college president's office, he thought of the worst possible things that could be about to happen to him. He was convinced that life was determined to deal him another blow. With dread he sat down in front of the president, who pushed a plain white envelope across the desk and told him to open it. In solemn silence he opened the envelope and took out what was inside—a check for $500.

"Who did this?" the student asked. In those days men did not cry, but by this time tears were running freely down his face.

"I can't tell you," explained the president. "I know the only thing they want in return is your service in God's kingdom."

In that moment the student would have done anything for the ones who had saved his financial life, not because he owed it to them, but because their love had awakened his love.

When Jesus said, "I have come that they might have life and have it more abundantly" (John 10:10), He was talking about people who expected the worst and had no protection against it. We are those people. As we sit in the president's office knowing we are a short lifetime away from losing our eternal souls, a white envelope is pushed toward us. For no other reason than that He loves us, the paper, on which we might have expected the worst blow to be written, is clean. All our debts have been forgiven. Is there anything we would not do for the One who saved us from eternal ruin?

Use whatever tools you need to motivate the change agents who can help promote your missions program in your church. Keep them in mind for the select group of people who will be your missions planning group, too. But remember, the greatest motivator is not a tool. "It is the love of Christ that controls us."

Forming the Core Group

Now we are going to look at what a missions planning group or missions com-mittee might look like. If you already have a missions committee you may want to compare what you have with what we see you ending up with. The following is a list of potential missions planning group members. We have tried to give you the profiles of those you might have, but the list is not exhaustive or even required. You may want to add more or you may feel comfortable with less. Try to fit our intentions with your reality.

Staff member. The senior minister's positive and productive contribution is essential. He need not be the chairperson, but he or one of the associate ministers should be active on the missions committee.

Long-time members. Someone who has served on the church's governing body and is respected by the church body. If possible try to find a man and a woman.

Young people. You are looking for change agents to fill these positions, so you may want one of the teenagers who seems to be the most active in his group.

New active members. Where possible, your missions committee should have at least 50% new members.

Prayer List

Possible candidates for members of this group (list)

_____

_____

_____

_____

Other concerns:

_____

_____

_____

_____

✧

Make a list of the people you believe would make the best candidates for your missions planning group. As you pray for the needs of the world, you can now pray for people who have within their control the power to meet those needs through the name of Jesus. It is always good to be specific in prayer.

✧

You may also want to recruit one person who is a part of an active and successful program in your church. He or she will bring some great ideas and energy to the program. The youth and the seniors are two other groups often overlooked when core groups are formed. You may also want to be sure you have a balance of men and women. Try to find the change agents for their particular groups.

The Spirit is able to use people because of what they are rather than who they are. Their position in the church does not qualify them to "set apart" ministers—their openness to cross-cultural ministry and their faithfulness to God's kingdom are their main qualifications.

Who is qualified to help accomplish work in your church? Who will hear the Spirit when He says, "Separate out for me"? These are the people you want to serve with you on the missions planning group.

One of the first things you will want to do is pray for other people in your church who can work with you to develop a missions program. As you begin to pray, talk about who you should consider as potential members of this missions planning group. Pray for their willingness to serve for that end.

How Long Will This Take?

The process you are about to begin is not a one-year project. In fact, it is not a project at all, but a way to fill your church with a climate in which missionaries can grow and people can use their gifts to reach God's world. If you follow it through to its final phase, the shortest amount of time you may expect it to take is five years. During that five-year period you will collect more workers, but the core group will be the catalyst for everything that happens between now and then.   ✦

✧

It may also be a good idea to ask the core group to enter into a covenant relationship. Here is a possible covenant you might agree together to keep.

✧

Covenant

Because our heavenly Father is a missionary God and because 'while we were still helpless, at the right time Christ died for me,' I will combine my will, gifts, and skills with the missions planning group or missions committee here for a minimum of one year and, with God's help, a maximum of five years.

_____

Chapter Three

Your Theology of Mission

WHAT DO YOU think God wants from His church? What are you personally willing to spend time doing in the name of the Lord? We all have a great deal to do to keep up with life. We must earn a living, which takes from 9 to 16 hours a day 5 to 6 days a week. If you are married and have children you will spend a good deal of the remaining time meeting their needs. If you are single you will often have other family or social group responsibilities to fill in the time. Along comes Joe Preacher, who says you need to give some of your time to God's work. You probably agree. But in which part of God's work are you going to labor?

The local church is in much the same situation. Regardless of where it may be located, whether in the sprawling urban complex or remote rural site, the church must look at its community in light of its resources. There is just not enough money or people-hours to fill all the needs in the community. How does the church decide where it will serve? Who will receive assistance and who will not? That decision might determine whether some people around your church will have food to eat that day or whether they must wait until tomorrow. In most cases the needy will eventually find another source of help and the church's decision will not have long-standing ramifications.

But when a church decides to send one missionary rather than another, it is also deciding who will hear the gospel and who will not. This is a decision that does have far-reaching consequences. And yet, far too many churches have little criteria for deciding what missionary they will support among the many that come to them asking for support. In many cases the missions committee will simply react to the many requests for help it receives —if a request is especially persuasive, or if the missionary is known personally by one of the committee members, or if they make a dynamic presentation to the committee, then a decision is made to help support them. Usually there is little or no active attempt to develop or help missionaries beyond the giving of money, or even to develop guidelines for which missionaries they will support.

How does the church make such an eternally important decision?

What Do You Believe?

If you were asked why you go to church, how would you respond?

- "Because I believe Jesus Christ is the Son of God and my Savior."
- "Because I believe the church is the community of believers united to help each other and the community in the name of Jesus."
- "Because I believe I cannot grow as a Christian unless I'm in God's house every Lord's day."

All of these are good answers. They will all lead you to actions that will bring you closer to God and His kingdom. However, they are different and will lead to different activities in His kingdom.

What we believe leads us to determine what we value. If you believe the simple process of putting a piece of metal into a hole and turning it will start a car, you will not question that process until something interferes to cause you to believe otherwise. If you borrow an unfamiliar car, for example, you will ask for the keys, believing they will start the car.

But then one day your car doesn't start. You go to a locksmith and say, "This key no longer starts my car. Would you sell me one that will?"

The locksmith replies, "Actually, it's the battery that starts the car. Why don't you buy a new battery?"

You now have two options. You may go to another locksmith who has the same belief as you and buy that new key. Or you may adjust your belief system to include the battery you had not realized was so important to the process. During the time you own your automobile, you will be faced with several of these times of decision. But each time you will not only learn something about how the car starts, but how to keep the car in condition so that it will start more often than it doesn't start.

We often operate the church in a similar fashion. We may believe that Jesus is the head of the church and that He wants good leadership to make it "start." If the church has good leaders it will start. There is a lot of truth in this belief. A church may start for years as a result of the intuitive ability of its leaders. But there will almost certainly come a time when that leadership cannot start the church. The members will go looking for new leaders to start the church, only to find they need something else altogether. They still need good leaders, but they also need good followers, good knowledge of the community, and good compassion for the lost.

The person who believed the key would start the car and the church that believed good leaders would start a church were, at first, satisfied. Just as the Keyite took good care of the key, the church took good care of its leaders. The Keyite probably had a special place for the key and polished it regularly. The church honored its leaders and gave them a special place in the body. They both acted on the basis of their belief. They would have been foolish not to. Neither was totally wrong. They would only have been wrong if they held no belief and merely accepted what was happening, making no plan to keep it starting.

When the church knows what it believes, it can plan to succeed in fulfilling God's mission. When its beliefs are revised due to further study, it will need to redraw its plan.

Now try an exercise to

✧

Here is an example showing how we arrived at our belief about the church.

The basic belief statement is in bold at the bottom of the box. It was based on the following Scripture passages: Luke 19:10; Colossians 1:24-29; Ephesians 3:10, 11; Acts 11:19-30; Acts 13:1-3

Now it's your turn. Using the list starting on the next page, write out your belief statements.

✧

The Church

In Luke 19:10 Jesus clearly states His purpose, which is to seek and save those who are lost. Colossians 1:24-29 makes it clear that the church is the body of Christ when Paul says, "Now I rejoice in what was suffered for you, and I fill up in my flesh what is still lacking in regard to Christ's afflictions, for the sake of His body, which is the church." Paul goes on to say he was commissioned to present the word of God to the Gentiles, "teaching everyone with all wisdom, so that we may present everyone perfect in Christ."

Ephesians 3:10, 11 adds to our knowledge when Paul points out, "His [God's] intent was that now, through the church, the manifold wisdom of God should be made known to the rulers and authorities in the heavenly realms, according to his eternal purpose which he accomplished in Christ Jesus our Lord."

We have a clear example of the church completing the work of Jesus in Acts 11:19-30 and 13:1-3. Here we see the church reaching out to people who do not know Jesus regardless of their language or nationality. Then we see the church sending out two of its best leaders to reach parts of the world most of the members would never be able to visit.

"I believe the church is the body of Christ and, like Him, its purpose is to 'seek and to save the lost.'"

help you identify your beliefs. Look at the list of subjects beginning on the next page and write down what you believe about each one. Your belief statements need not be as complete as the example we have provided below.

For each topic we have listed several key Scripture passages that can help you write your belief statements. You are free to use them or add Scripture references you feel are pertinent in defining your belief statement. Your belief statements may be broader than the Scriptures listed, but don't try to be too complex. Belief statements are best when they are short enough to be memorized. The statement you write should accurately reflect what you really believe about that topic.

If we have left out one or two subjects you would like to address, use the blank boxes at the end of the list to complete your study.

This may take you several hours to complete. If you are doing this with a group, it would be best if you completed this exercise on your own and then compared it with the group.

The Savior

✧

Regarding the Savior, I believe:

Mark 10:45;
John 1:29;
John 3:16;
Colossians 1:15-20;
1 Timothy 2:3-6

✧

The Sinful World

✧

Regarding the sinful world, I believe:

Isaiah 53:6;
Romans 3:23;
Romans 6:23;
Romans 8:5-8

✧

*Regarding the
Scripture, I believe:*

*2 Timothy 3:16;
1 Thessalonians 2:13;
Hebrews 4:12;
2 Peter 1:20,21*

Scripture

*Regarding spiritual
leaders, I believe:*

*Mark 10:42-45;
Acts 6:2-4;
1 Thessalonians 2:1-12;
1 Timothy 3:1-13;
2 Timothy 2:1-7, 14-16;
Titus 1:5-9;
1 Peter 5:1-4*

Spiritual Leaders

*Regarding suffering,
I believe:*

*Luke 6:20-26;
John 16:33;
Acts 14:22;
Romans 5:3-5;
Philippians 1:29;
Hebrews 12:2, 3;
1 Peter 1:6
1 Peter 2:19-21;
1 Peter 4:12-19*

Suffering

Salvation

✦

*Regarding salvation,
I believe:*

*John 3:16;
John 5:24;
Acts 4:12;
Romans 10:8-13;
Ephesians 2:8, 9;
2 Peter 3:9*

✦

Stewardship

✦

*Regarding stewardship
(time, energy,
possessions), I
believe:*

*Psalm 24:1;
Matthew 6:33;
Mark 12:29-31;
Luke 12:42-48;
Acts 2:41-47;
Acts 4:32-37;
2 Corinthians 9:6-8*

✦

Social Involvement

✦

*Regarding social
involvement, I believe:*

*Proverbs 21:13;
Proverbs 29:7;
Matthew 25:31-46;
Luke 4:18, 19;
Luke 14:12-14;
Galatians 6:9;
James 1:27—2:13;
1 John 3:16-18*

✦

Regarding spiritual
power (the Holy Spirit,
angels, demons),
I believe:

Mark 11:22-24;
Acts 1:8;
2 Corinthians 10:3, 4;
Ephesians 6:10-18;
Philippians 4:13;
1 John 4:1-8

Spiritual Power

Regarding spiritual
disciplines (prayer,
Bible study), I believe:

Joshua 1:8;
Luke 5:16;
Acts 2:42;
1 Thessalonians 5:17;
1 Timothy 4:12-16;
2 Timothy 2:15

Spiritual Disciplines

Use this space and the
space on the next
page to address any
subjects you feel we
have left out.

Use this space to address any subject you feel we have left out.

Now you can tell your friends you have written your own personal theology. You are now a theologian! Do you feel any different? Probably not, though you should have a sense of accomplishment. Not everyone has a clear statement of their beliefs, even though they operate on a definite system of beliefs. The difference is that you have your theology where you can examine it. Before you decide to become active in a local civic group, or start a Bible study, or form a missions committee, you can begin by saying, "In light of my theology I will make the following decision."

Let's say a member of the church asks, "Why do we have adult Sunday schools? Where is that in the Bible?" We would go back to our belief statement and say, "In light of the fact that we believe the church is the body of Christ, and like Him, its purpose is to 'seek and to save the lost,' we want to train our adult members to know the head of the church and be prepared to reach out to the unsaved." If our adult Sunday school is not in line with this statement, we have two choices. We can either change our belief statement through further study of the Word of God, or we can change our adult Sunday school.

Time Out!

If you have been doing this with a core group, you will want to take some time to compare notes. You should also spend some time combining your insights on each topic. When you have done this you have written a theology your group can use as a basis for further work.

As you work through the rest of this book, you will frequently want to look back to these belief statements. When you make a decision to institute a program, come back to your belief statements to review and evaluate your decision in light of your theology.

Don't misunderstand us. We are not suggesting you write a creed and then require all prospective members abide by a man-made document. We are suggesting you should have a working document that allows you to compare what you are doing with what you believe. Examine it often. Change it as you grow in your study and understanding. But whatever you do, use it.   ◆

Chapter Four

Your Present Program

Have you ever been asked why you do something the way you do? As you thought about it, you might have realized you were not sure why. Your best answer may have been, "Because it seemed like the right thing to do," or even, "I don't know, that's the way I've always done it." Our philosophy of life is often something we use rather than something we understand.

In its simplest form, the term, "philosophy of . . ." refers to how we carry out our beliefs given our particular context. If you were asked why you own a car, it might not occur to you to answer, "Because I believe I should be able to go from one place to another whenever I wish without having to rely on another person to transport me." But that would probably be an accurate statement of your belief and the reason why you own a car.

The same basic belief might be expressed in different ways depending on your context. If you lived in New York City, where parking a car costs as much as buying one, you might apply your philosophy in a different way. From the same basic belief you might say, "In light of my right to get from one place to another at will and given the realities of my community, I will learn to use the public transportation system and use the money saved from parking garages to buy a bicycle for shorter journeys." In another country we might, given the same belief, rely on boats, airplanes, or foot paths.

In this chapter you'll be working backwards, looking at the existing programs of your church and evaluating them in the light of the theological beliefs you wrote down in the last chapter. You will be testing your church activities to see whether they are in line with your theology of missions.

You will find a shopping list of programs below to help you understand what we mean when we talk about programs. Circle or highlight the programs now funcioning in your church, and add any that we didn't mention.

✧

Look at the list and circle or highlight the programs that now exist in your church. Space is provided for you to add programs we have not listed. Don't check any of the boxes yet—those are for the next step.

✧

Programs of Your Church

❑ Calling
❑ Graded Sunday school
❑ Senior saints
❑ Leadership training
❑ Prayer warriors
❑ College/career class
❑ Day care
❑ Christian school
❑ Women's Bible study
❑ Short term missions trips
❑ Choir
❑ Mid-week Bible study
❑ Prison ministry
❑ Quilting group
❑ Fellowship dinners
❑ Deaf ministry
❑ Literary or arts group

❑ Preschool
❑ Youth groups
❑ Soup kitchen
❑ Support groups
❑ Nursery
❑ Singles
❑ Counseling
❑ Sports activities
❑ Men's Bible study
❑ Holiday cantatas
❑ Sunday worship
❑ Cell group Bible study
❑ Bus ministry
❑ Political action group
❑ Vacation Bible School
❑ Building committee
❑ Ministry with handicapped persons

Others (list below)

❑ _____

❑ _____

❑ _____

❑ _____

Now go back to your belief statements and read them. Then look at each program of your church and evaluate it in the light of your belief statements.

As an example, in the last chapter we wrote a belief statement about the church: "We believe the church is the body of Christ, and, like Him, its purpose is to seek and to save the lost." In the light of that belief statement, let's look at a program in our church that centers around feeding the poor. Why do we have this program? Should our church be using its limited resources to feed the poor when its primary purpose, according to our statement of belief, is to be the body of Jesus Christ and to seek and save the lost?

To come to a resolution on this issue, we need to first look at how our head, Jesus, treated the hungry. If we assume that Jesus' theology was the Great Commission, we can also assume He fed the 5000 and the 4000 for a purpose. Was that purpose to give the people a meal? To demonstrate God's love and care? To illustrate that He is the Bread of Life? Or all of the above?

Depending on our environment and our resources, we might decide this program should be continued

as it is, or that it should be dropped, or that it needs to be refocused so that the church could see our belief in the program and the community could see our heart in our actions.

Put a check beside the programs that are integral to fulfilling your theology of mission. It is best to do this with the whole group participating. You should expect to spend at least an hour on this process, since there will be some serious discussion.

Interpreting the Results

If you checked *all the programs* presently used in your church, then you're doing everything right. Whether by accident or design, your theology is being lived out in the decisions of the church. You are intentional and purposeful in fulfilling your theology of mission.

If you checked *some but not all,* then congratulations. Some of your church's programs are purposeful in fulfilling your theology of mission. However, you have said that the other programs are not helping to fulfill that mission.

There are two possibilities why a program may not be fulfilling a church's mission. First, it may be that the

program has not been used appropriately and needs to be rethought and adapted to your theology. Second, it may be that you're looking at a perfectly good concept that could not be carried out in your context. For a program to work in the church, it is something you believe you should do, something you have the resources to do, and something you can feel good about doing.

Let's look again at the illustration of feeding the poor. We might find two churches with the same belief but different applications. One will express their belief by becoming an active supporter of a local agency that is geared up for large scale assistance. Their primary resource in this area is money. Another church may respond to the same belief by opening a soup kitchen in the basement and calling on volunteers to staff it on a weekly basis. Neither church is more righteous than the other. One is operating on the philosophy that specialization is the most efficient way to minister while the other holds to the philosophy that local involvement shows mercy.

Go back and look at each of the programs in your church that you did not check. What was the reason you didn't check it? Was it because the program didn't work in your situation (but it could work under other conditions), or was it because the program would not fulfill your missions theology no matter how you applied it?

If you checked *only a few or none* of your programs, then you are like a ship lying dead in the water. If you are a new congregation, you probably have not even left the harbor. Because your programs do not reflect your theology you are operating at cross purposes. You believe one thing but are doing another.

You will need to do one of two things. You could re-think your theology in light of your programs and decide you are more comfortable with the theology you are doing than the one you are saying. Or you could change your programming and bring it into line with your theology. (We recommend the latter option over the former.)

You have just examined your theology of mission and examined your current church programs in the light of that theology. Now you know where you are, and you have a better idea of where you're going. If you just confirmed what you already knew, congratulations! That happens all too rarely in this world. If you just decided you needed to scrap some of what you've been doing, congratulations! You have found out about the problem and you know what the solution is. That is also rare in this world.

Now we are ready to set some goals and plan some strategies. Let's go!　　　✦

Chapter Five

Your Missions Goals

NOW THAT YOU'VE identified your theology of mission (Chapter 3) and examined the programs now functioning in your church (Chapter 4), you're now ready to begin to move beyond where you are in your mission and in your missions program.

You face a great temptation at this point. You are tempted to get right to work in planning what to do and what programs and activities to start. You do need to have specific programs and activities that will help grow the missions program of your church. Beginning with this chapter you will work toward establishing or expanding your church's missions program. But before we talk about specific program ideas or strategies, we need to identify what we're trying to accomplish.

A goal is something you reach for, and a strategy is something you do to accomplish your goal. In this chapter you'll do some dreaming and identify where you'd like your missions program to be someday. You'll set a direction and establish some large-scale priorities. In this chapter you'll try to answer the question, "Where are we going?" We'll save the "How will we get there?" and "What are we going to do?" questions for the next chapter.

Let us illustrate the difference between goals and

Key Missions Goals

1. Build a strong churchwide missions prayer support.
2. Provide consistent missions education and develop world Christians.
3. Involve church members in cross-cultural evangelism and ministry.
4. Equip missions leaders and missionary recruits for effective service.
5. Mobilize the congregation to support (wholistically) and send missionaries.
6. Develop a long-range plan (5 or 6 years) to accomplish the above goals.
7. Write a missions policy.
8. Mobilize other churches to be missions-active churches.

✧

These suggested goals provide not only an example of how to write goals, but also identify the critical goals for a well-rounded missions program. The goals listed have some sense of priority and sequence.

✧

strategies. One of the authors has set as a family goal to be personally involved in cross-cultural ministry. This goal is simple, it's achievable, and it can be measured. But many strategies could be employed to be personally involved in cross-cultural ministry. Here are some strategies we have chosen to accomplish that goal:

- hosting an international student
- participating in short-term mission projects
- praying for and writing to missionaries
- making lifestyle changes to financially support world mission

Only when you know where you want to go can you make deliberate choices as to how to get there. Clarifying your goals determines what strategies or programs you will use.

The authors, in their work with church missions programs, have identified several key goals that create a growing, healthy, and biblically based missions program. We list them above not as the only possible set of missions goals that churches should adopt, but we do suggest that these are basic goals you will want to consider. You must decide on your own goals, based on your theology of mission, your

current strengths and weaknesses, and how you believe God is leading your church in world mission.

The goal-setting process is to be done seeking the leading and guidance of the Holy Spirit. Schedule significant time in personal and corporate prayer before and during the process of goal setting.

Your own goals may come out different than these. That can be expected, since each church is unique. At the same time your goals may sound similar; that too would be expected, since the same basic components make up every church that is active and effective in accomplishing God's mission in the world.

Now it's your turn to get to work. Your action project is to write your own goals. Look over the sample goals presented. Consider and brainstorm with your planning team where you want your church to be in its missions outreach so that you can answer the question, "Where are we going?" You should be able to state a goal in one sentence. It should be stated as an action and be simple and clear. Be careful not to write too many or too few goals. Keep them clear and focused.　　　　✦

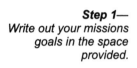

Step 1—
Write out your missions goals in the space provided.

Set Your Goals

Rewrite the Goals

Example: *Because we believe that* the church is the body of Christ, and, like Him, its purpose is to seek and save the lost, *we therefore want to* involve our church members in some form of cross-cultural evangelism and ministry.

Step 2—
Rewrite your goals in the space provided, making sure they tie into your theology of mission (Chapter 3). Do this by taking the goals you've written and adding a phrase at the beginning of the sentence like, "Because we . . ." or "In light of . . ." In the example we started with our belief statement about the church from Chapter 3 and have established a goal based on that belief.

Step 3—
Now prioritize your goals. Which goals are most important?

Now you're ready to discuss how you're going to accomplish these goals. But before you move on to the next chapter, you might also want to consider how you'll communicate these goals to the key leaders of your church and to the entire congregation. Be creative! Answer the following questions about how you'll communicate your missions goals.

Communicate the Goals

Who needs to know? Identify specific groups in your congregation that you'll target (Bible school classes, church staff, elders, church board, ministry groups, small groups)

How will you tell them? (church newsletter, printed materials, personal presentation, audiovisual presentation, skits, sermons, lessons)

When and how often will you communicate these goals?

Chapter Six

Your Missions Strategies

Y OU'RE NOW READY to decide how you'll accomplish your goals by identifying strategies (also called programs or action steps) for each goal you've written. Then after you've decided on strategies for each of your goals, you'll coordinate them into one complete Missions Mobilization Plan.

Make copies of the blank worksheet on page 39. Give each person in your missions planning group a set of the blank worksheets, one for each goal you set in Chapter 5. Fill in the top of each page by transferring your goals to these sheets (one goal per sheet). Under each goal is the statement, "In order to fulfill this goal we will do the following:"

You can determine your strategies by considering these three possibilities for strategy choice:

- Identify programs that currently exist that will fulfill the goal (you might want to refer back to Chapter 4).
- Identify programs that need to be adjusted, changed, or dropped to fulfill the goal.
- Consider adding new programs or strategies that will fulfill the goal.

Appendix A contains a list of missions strategies by major category, with resources available to help you. You might want to review this appendix for additional strategy ideas.

Missions Goal

In order to fulfill this goal we will do the following:

Strategy, Program, or Action Step	Leaders	Time Frame	Resources Needed	Contributing Factors

For each worksheet, work together and determine your strategies according to these steps:

Step 1—In the left-hand column, list the strategies you might choose to accomplish the goal.

Step 2—Prioritize your strategies on the worksheet by placing a number or letter by each one. Decide which strategies are most important and need immediate attention, planning, and resource allocation.

Step 3—Identify possible leadership for each strategy in the second column. Somebody has to "own" each particular strategy or program or it will simply remain an idea on paper. Who will take ownership and get the ball rolling, even if it's just to delegate the job to someone else?

Step 4—In the third column, schedule your mission strategy or program. Include a specific starting point and a projected time frame. Be sure to coordinate these with your church calendar. You can always revise the starting time and duration, but the key is to plan one. Many programs never get started because no decision is made on when to start.

Step 5—In the fourth column, begin discussing specific resources needed. The leader(s) of the particular action step or program will have to be more detailed and specific about the program. At this point you simply want to consider if there are significant resources needed that will have to be planned for or that would inhibit the implementation of that program idea.

In the last column you can add any other pertinent information.

Step 6—You will find it helpful to review these planning sheets every six months or more often. Evaluation and accountability are essential to insure that the time and effort put into planning will result in real and meaningful change in your missions program.

On the next page is a sample of how your goal and strategy worksheet might look.

A Missions Mobilization Plan

Now that you've come up with some strategies, you probably have more than you can implement in any given year. You need to put all these strategies into a workable multi-year plan. Some strategies you will

want to use on a regular or annual basis, and others you will want to use only after you've prepared the way for their acceptance.

For instance, let's say one of your goals concerns missions education and you've decided that one of your strategies is to have a missions education conference every eighteen months. Another goal is to identify and develop candidates for missionary service over several years, and you've listed several strategies for that. A third goal is to involve a wide cross-section of your congregation in part-time or short-term missions work. One of your strategies for this goal is to go on a one-week mission trip to Mexico, taking people from your congregation interested in missions.

You need to plot these strategies along with any others into a multi-year calendar so that you have a balanced and manageable plan. We call this a Missions Mobilization Plan (MMP), because it sets the course for mobilizing your church in missions.

Remember that the purpose for all your work is to create an environment in your church in which you can recruit, equip, send, shepherd, and support missionaries. It has been the

Missions Goal #3

Because we believe that the church is the body of Christ, and like Jesus, its purpose is to seek and save the lost, we therefore want to involve our church members in some form of cross-cultural evangelism and ministry.

In order to fulfill this goal, we will do the following:

Strategy, Program, or Action Step	Leaders	Time Frame	Resources Needed	Contributing Factors
1. Provide a short-term cross-cultural missions project to a place where we currently support a missionary.	Associate minister; mission chairman	18 months from today's date	Contact missions to determine options	Annual missions meeting 20 months from today
2. Establish an international student-host ministry	George Johnson and campus chaplain	Begin the fall of next school year	Campus ministry resources	Interest in campus ministry
3. Investigate and develop a discipleship and evangelism ministry in a low-income urban housing project	John and Mary Doe	Begin now to investigate --report done in 2 months	Unknown	Local and low cost
4. Create a plan to allow church families (other than staff and Missions Committee) to house and/or feed furlough missionaries over the next 18 months	Minister; Helen Jones	Plan to cover the next 18 months	-------	Relationship w/Hospitality Committee

A Sample Missions Mobilization Plan

This is an example of how strategies can be scheduled into a six-year plan. Just think, in six years you can send cross-cultural missionaries to participate in the task of world evangelism!

Year One
- First prayer group formed
- First missions education conference (focus: Unreached Peoples)
- Bulletin inserts every six weeks
- Church mission awareness survey results reported
- Discipling leaders recruited and trained
- Key leaders sent to missions conferences

Year Two
- First short-term missions project
- Second missions education conference (focus: Personal Involvement in World Mission)
- Bible school mission emphasis leaders developed
- Christmas in July instituted
- First discipling groups formed
- Weekend urban ministry projects

Year Three
- Second short-term missions project
- Adult Bible school elective, "Becoming World Christians"
- Faith Promise initiated
- Missionary recruit preparation guide completed
- Missionary recruit shepherding groups formed
- New discipleship groups formed
- Missions publicity takes higher profile

Years Four and Five
- Short-term project to a target field of recruits
- Sermon series on world evangelism
- Recruit shepherding groups—individual preparation plans now in progress
- Research on destination fields
- Continuation and expansion of already existing programs

Year Six
- Confirm recruits' preparation
- Finalize funding plans
- Plan sending/commissioning services
- Send first mission team to field
- Establish detailed support and shepherding plans
- Evaluation and future plans for world evangelization

experience of the authors that the average American congregation will need around six years to fully develop that kind of environment that can raise up and send missionaries. But your good intentions may not be realized if you fail to develop and follow a plan of action. A plan is essential if we want to utilize the power of God. Your plans must be taken seriously, they must be flexible, and they must be reviewed regularly.

Maybe your current goals and strategies will not fill out a complete MMP like the example provided. Don't let that deter you from filling one out as completely as possible. An MMP is flexible enough to add to, delete from, or change upon regular review. It becomes your key document that maps out your missions program for the next several years. It is your primary planning and evaluation tool.

When you've completed your planning pages, use this sample MMP to help you schedule your strategies over a four- to six-year period. ✦

Chapter Seven

Your Missions Leadership

A MISSIONS COMMIT-tee can function in two basic ways, creating two different types of missions programs.

The Decision-Making Committee sees itself as delegated to run the missions program of the church for everyone else. It makes financial decisions, decides on requests from missionaries, and plans a yearly missions conference. Its emphasis is on decisions about what to contribute financially to missions. The missions program focuses on the support of existing missionaries. The decision-making committee usually meets once a month. Often members serve for one-year terms.

The Missions-Active Committee has assigned each member of the committee a key area of missions leadership (or a subcommittee) like missions education, missions strategy, recruitment and candidate preparation, short-term missions, or missions prayer. Members of this committee have an ownership of their part of the missions program and view it as their primary ministry and service. Its emphasis is on how to mobilize, stimulate, and involve the church to evangelize the world. It has a special concern for sending new missionaries in addition to supporting existing ones. The missions-active committee meets anywhere from once a week to twice a month. Membership is usually long-term.

The missions-active committee will involve your church in missions and move it to accomplish its mission. A key to establishing a missions-active committee is to assign current members and/or recruit new members to lead or serve on a sub-committee or perform a specific assignment. This insures an "active" focus rather than a "decision-making" focus. This will also help to create owner-ship and long-term stability, as well as move beyond getting things decided to actually getting things done!

You must be aware of your key players and find ways to equip and en-courage them in the role they play in growing your missions program. Below are some possible things to consider in mobilizing the various people who will lead in missions. Not every category of persons will be covered, only those that most frequently are respon-sible for moving and grow-ing your missions program. Be sure that you have made a plan of how to train and equip your key mis-sions leadership if you want

your church to be a part of evangelizing the world.

Equipping and Training

Some preliminary as-sumptions need to be examined before address-ing the practical way mis-sions committee members are equipped.

First, *being precedes doing*. In recruiting new members it's essential to look for potential in people who are (or can be) faithful disciples, world Christians, informed about missions, and who will actively lead in your missions outreach. Who they are (their being) will determine largely the effectiveness of what they contribute (their doing).

Second, you must *trust God to develop people*. True transformation of people ultimately comes as the Holy Spirit convicts, molds, and transforms the believer. God can and will transform people into the image of His Son. Pray fervently for your existing and future committee mem-bers' personal growth.

The missions committee chairperson must be com-mitted to allowing time, energy, and resources for the training and equipping of committee members. This commitment on the chairperson's part is essen-tial. His or her expectations

of the members will keep training a priority, which is often lost in all the "urgent" business. Trained and equipped committee mem-bers are vitally important if you're going to deal effec-tively with all the urgent missions business!

We equip and train people in two basic ways—the formal and informal processes. An effective training program will use both.

The *formal process* of training and equipping might include the follow-ing:

- attendance at mission conferences (funding provided?)
- committee devotions or studies
- committee training time (each meeting, monthly, quarterly)
- committee retreats
- new committee member orientation
- reading reports

The most cost-efficient in terms of time and resources is the informal method. In-formal training is the equip-ping that occurs as a "by-product" of various circum-stances and experiences. For example, you can train your committee members as you develop a missions policy (see Chapter 8). Your goal is to create a missions policy to guide your missions program, but a by-product of that can be the missions education of your committee members. As you discuss major missions policy categories you can provide teaching, readings, or biblical study about that area. You might also assign people to do a first draft policy of an area and suggest resources and Scriptures they might research. The discussion about the policies by the committee members can also be informal training as missions principles, strategies, and biblical concepts are addressed. The key is for the leader to look for ways to maximize the informal training options available.

Don't be discouraged if your committee members have a long way to go. Every long journey begins with the first step! Go ahead and take your first step now.

Identify here how you'll approach equipping the missions committee.

✧

Equipping the Missions Committee

Step 1—What do the committee members need in terms of orientation, training, and equipping?

Step 2—What strategies (formal and informal) can we use to respond to these needs?

Step 3—What resources will help us accomplish these training needs?

Step 4—Who are potential committee members that we will pray for regarding their recruitment? What would be their potential assignment?

Questions About Your Church Leadership

Do you know how the leaders view missions? How will you find out?

How will the missions committee work with the leaders? What is the current relationship like?
How would you or the leaders like it to be?

How involved will these leaders be in the missions program of the church, and in what ways?

Minister and Church Staff

Your church staff, especially the main preaching/leading minister, is the key to the success of your program. If they are truly supportive and committed to world evangelism, then God can do great things in your church. If they are resistant or apathetic, then your missions committee will find it is handicapped in its ability to involve and mobilize the entire church in world mission. What follows are some suggestions about how to get your staff "on board" if they currently are not. We are grateful for much of our thinking on this subject to Woody Phillips, Jr., mission pastor of Church of the Savior in Wayne, Pennsylvania.

- Pray for your staff.
- Involve them in decision making.
- Send them on short-term mission projects or to visit missionaries.
- Give them mission resources.
- Don't expect them to come up with ideas and programs (committee members can do that), but involve them effectively in those programs.
- Spend time with the staff, learning about their views of missions.

Here's how the staff can help the missions program. The staff must . . .

- promote and teach about missions in their areas of ministry.
- give time for missions programs in the regular services/meetings.
- not treat missions as a separate concern, but tie missions to the mission of God for the church.
- keep missions (like evangelism, discipleship, and worship) on the front burner the entire year.

Leadership or Governing Body

Given the answers to the questions about your church leadership on the previous page, we make five suggestions that will help build a solid team approach to missions:

1. Have key leaders of the missions committee talk with church leaders about these questions.

2. Have church leaders serve on or chair the missions committee.

3. When developing or evaluating a missions policy and goals, be sure to involve the leadership before a final copy is produced. The leadership should also "own" the policy and goals. You can build into your missions policy the answers to some of the questions on the previous page.

4. Consistently pray for the vision of your church leadership.

5. The principles and ideas in the previous section on church staff may apply also to the leadership.

Other Key Leaders

We suggest these ideas to equip, train, and involve other leaders in your church.

1. Missionary candidates and recruits are a key source of leadership for the missions program.

2. Educate new church members about your missions program. Is missions highlighted in new member materials and in their orientation programs?

3. Utilize missionaries and mission agency personnel for consultations and training in your missions program. ✦

Chapter Eight

Your Missions Policy

CONSIDER THE FOLlowing scenario. It's the annual budget meeting for the missions committee. You will spend hours discussing which missionaries to add, which ones to drop, and which ones will have increased support or decreased support. In addition to missionary support, you will also discuss the agencies, educational institutions, benevolence, and social programs to be considered.

Every year someone wants to add or increase support for a particular concern. It's usually a frustrating process, because there are no guidelines by which to make decisions regarding your limited missions dollars. The missions chairperson has a gloomy outlook on this year's meeting because of last year's fight over dropping one mission agency and the heated discussion over the role of social programs. In fact, one missions committee

member quit in anger after last year's budget meeting. The chairperson wonders if there is any way to avoid this confusion and frustration each year.

Budgeting decisions are just one reason why it's important to have a missions policy for your church. Here are some additional reasons for having a missions policy:

1. A missions policy gives broad guidelines that set a direction and keep the

Missions Policy Outline

We suggest that a comprehensive missions policy might include the following sections.

Preamble and/or Purpose
    Definition of missions (refer to Chapter 1)
    Scriptural support for missions (refer to Chapter 3)
    Priority of missions

Missions Committee
    Purpose
    Responsibilities of the committee and individual members
    Goal-setting guidelines
    Selection of members
    Organization and officers
    Role of the church staff and leadership

Missions Policy
    Evaluation
    Revision
    Approval
    Interpretation

The Church's Responsibility to Missions
    Prayer
    Shepherding
    Financial support
    Other support (furlough, education, retirement, etc.)
    Reporting and communication
    Visitation

The Church's Responsibility to Missions Candidates and Recruits
    Definitions
    Preparation, training, equipping, education
    Shepherding
    Approval and confirmation
    Financial considerations

Responsibilities of the Missionaries, Missions Agencies, and Other Organizations to the Church
    Reporting
    Meeting with the church

Selection and Evaluation of Missionaries, Missions Agencies, and Other Organizations
    Criteria for qualification
    Selection process
    Evaluation process
    How to apply for consideration

Church Awareness and Stimulation

Short-term Missions Service
    Purpose
    Finances
    Preparation and follow-up
    Who qualifies to participate

Budget and Financial Guidelines
    Priorities in budgeting
    Budget preparation

main things as the main things without strangling or binding the committee's efforts to evangelize the world.

2. A missions policy that is carefully developed and "owned" by the entire committee, staff, and church leadership will provide a guide so that valuable time and energy is not wasted re-discussing the same issues.

3. A policy clarifies the who, what, and why responsibilities of the church and the missionary/agency.

4. A policy helps insure continuity from year to year, even if there are changes in the committee, staff, or church leadership.

5. It helps override individual preferences or requests not consistent with your theology or goals in missions.

6. The policy will help you communicate to the entire church why certain decisions were made.

7. The process of developing a policy can build cohesiveness to a missions committee and its program; it can provide valuable training for the committee members, church leaders, and even the staff.

Allow yourself plenty of time to develop your policy. Clovernook Christian Church in Cincinnati,

Ohio took over two years to complete theirs. The committee completed one section at a time and passed it on to the elders so they also could devote time to discussing it (to get the entire draft at once would have been difficult to discuss, assimilate, and own). The goal is not just to finish the policy, but to create ownership of a usable document that will guide your missions program as well as use the process for informal missions education. ✦

✧

Define Key Areas

Step 1—
Using the categories above, along with information from the ACMC Church Missions Policy Handbook and other church missions policies, begin writing your own outline. What subjects will need attention now and in the near future? In the space provided, brainstorm (without initial evaluation) a list. Then finalize the key topics or areas to be considered in your missions policy.

✧

Step 2—
*Decide how you'll
approach preparing
each section. Here are
some ideas.*

Decide on Your Approach

- Research what others have done for each section
- Identify official or unofficial policies and practices already operating in that area
- Assign a person or group to do a rough draft of each section
- Brainstorm the committee's, staff's, or leadership's concerns for each section
- Determine the approval process with other governing bodies, to include or involve them at appropriate points

Decide now how you'll approach this project:

Step 3—
*Set a schedule or
timetable to complete
the project. Expect to
revise your schedule
as you go.*

Set a Timetable

Obtain Approval

✧

Step 4—
Complete and obtain tentative approvals for each section. Who needs to give approval of your missions policy?

✧

Decide How You Will Communicate

✧

Step 5—
Upon completion, decide how you will communicate these policies to the church, missionaries, and missions agencies.

✧

Plan to Evaluate

✧

Step 6—
Plan to evaluate your policy at a future date. Determine how often such evaluation and revisions should occur and by whom.

✧

Conclusion

Completing the Journey

CONGRATULATIONS! you've just completed the planning stages of your missions program. But three vital steps are ahead: implementation, evaluation, and mobilization.

Implementation. A great plan that's not put into action is worthless. It's a waste of your time and effort. Be intentional about putting your plans into action. Create an accountability system in your missions committee. Review your plans regularly. Ask for reports from those who are responsible for various strategies and programs.

Evaluation. Schedule times now to evaluate your plans on a regular basis. How far have you come? What have you learned? What needs to be changed? What new needs have occurred? How far do you still have to go? Are your goals and strategies adequate?

Mobilization. Multiplication has always been God's plan to advance the gospel. As your church grows to become actively involved in the evangelization of the world, you will no doubt have learned many things that you could share with other churches. Actively consider how you'll encourage, motivate, and share your journey with others. Mobilizing other churches will multiply your own efforts. No church alone can evangelize the world, but together the churches that belong to Jesus Christ can finish the task. ◆

You and World Mission

✧

Now is an appropriate time for you to restate the purpose of your church in relationship to world evangelization.

How do you now see your involvement in world mission? Write your thoughts down now in the space provided.

✧

Encourage Other Churches

✧

Write down in the space provided the names of other churches that you can encourage and share your story with, and begin praying for an opportunity to do so. Consider passing this resource book along to them.

✧

Strategies and Program Ideas

These are strategies and program ideas to help you grow an effective missions program in your church. The first section has ideas for missions education and materials for equipping and training missions committee members and missionary recruits.

Missions Education

Developing World Christians
- Missions conferences (adults, youth, and children)
- Adult Bible school electives
- Missions self-evaluation
- Newsletter articles
- Bulletin inserts about the missionaries
- Guest missionary speakers
- Discipleship groups (also called growth groups, these are intensive training groups that focus on equipping believers with spiritual disciplines and skills to be disciple makers.)

- Missions resources available at your church: books, tracts, videos, magazines, films
- Christmas in September (Any month can be a time to remember and support missionaries by sending gifts. Mail early so they receive the gifts before Christmas.)
- Simulation games
- Sermons
- Missions speakers
- Bible school missions emphasis leaders

Equipping Key Missions Leaders and Missions Recruits
- Missionary recruit preparation and shepherding
- Missions conferences and seminars
- The Perspectives Course (A comprehensive missions education course provided through the U.S. Center for World Mission; see Appendix B)
- Church internships
- Formal education or studies on missions
- Informal training (like developing a missions policy)
- Shepherding groups for missionary candidates
- Host missions seminars at your church

Missionary Support

Supporting and Shepherding Missionaries
- Furlough assistance (transportation, housing, meals, etc.)
- Write and call missionaries
- Yearly reports (written or verbal)
- Field visits
- Prayer Sevens (see below)

Prayer
- Small weekly missions prayer groups
- Monthly churchwide missions prayer meetings
- Prayer Sevens (groups of seven people who each agree to take one day of the week to pray for a particular

✧

"Wholistic" support for missionaries includes prayer and personal support. This section will give you some ideas.

✧

missionary or missions recruit, involving many people in prayer for world missions and ensuring that every missionary and recruit is being supported in daily prayer.)
- Prayer seminars
- Prayer guides for the weekly bulletin or newsletter
- Concerts of prayer

Congregational Financing and Sending of Missionaries
- Faith promise
- Barnabas teams (A Barnabas team is made up of six to ten families who voluntarily simplify their lives so that they can give between $100-300 a month above their current giving. This team takes personal responsibility for financial support of the missionaries they know and love.)
- Percentage of the general church budget

Here are some ways to actively involve members of your congregation in missions beyond just the giving of money.

Membership Involvement

Cross-Cultural Evangelism and Ministry
- Urban or ethnic missions projects (weekend, weekly, etc.)
- International student ministry
- Short-term missions projects (adult and youth)
- Local evangelism and training involvement
- Mailing Bibles

Visual Reminders—Publicity
- Flags or maps of nations
- Bulletin boards
- Church newsletter or bulletin inserts
- Missionary pictures mounted on wall with current newsletter

Mobilizing Other Churches
- Area missions fellowship
- Joint sponsorship of a missionary
- ACMC (See Appendix B)

Appendix B

Resources by Topic

General Resources

Resource Lists
Appendix of *In the Gap,* David Bryant, ed. Regal Books.
Mission Resource Manual. U.S. Center for World Mission
Recommended Reading on the World Mission of the Church.
    InterVarsity Missions
The Updated Missions Tools and Resource Catalogue.
    InterVarsity Missions
Missions Resource Center. Call 1-800-TASK-ONE

Here and on the following page are missions resource books and organizations. Included are many of the addresses and telephone numbers for the resources listed in this section.

Organizations

Association of Church Missions Committees (ACMC)
P.O. Box ACMC, Wheaton, IL 60189-8000
1-800-798-ACMC (for orders) or (708) 260-1660

TASK ONE—Knoxville, TN
Call 1-800-827-5663 (1-800-TASK-ONE)
An organization to help churches mobilize in sending cross-
    cultural missionaries. They have planning consultants,
    resources, and networking available to help your church
    become missions-active. Established by the Missions
    Task Force of the Christian Churches/Churches of Christ.

U.S. Center for World Missions
1605 Elizabeth St., Pasadena, CA 91104
(818) 398-2200
Current research, publications, library, *Perspectives* Course

InterVarsity Missions
6400 Schroeder Rd., Box 7895, Madison, WI 53707-7895
(608) 274-9001
Videos, films, slides, books and publications, URBANA '90
    conference, short-term missions

Missions Advanced Research and Communication Center
    (MARC)
919 W. Huntington Drive, Monrovia, CA 91016
(818) 303-8811

Lausanne Committee for World Evangelization
P.O. Box 2270, Monrovia, CA 91017
(818) 303-8811
Publications and videos

Conferences

Urbana Conferences
P.O. Box 7895, Madison, WI 53707-7895
(608) 274-7883

ACMC Conference (see above for address)

Missions Education

Missions Education Handbook. ACMC.
A Disciple's Bifocals series (3-unit curriculum). ACMC.

World Christians
David Bryant, ed. *In the Gap.* Regal Books.
David Bryant, *A World Christian Check-up.* InterVarsity
    Missions.
Paul Borthwick, *A Mind for Missions.* Navpress.
J. Herbert Kane, *Wanted: World Christians.* Baker.
World Christian (magazine), P.O. Box 40010, Pasadena, CA
    91114.
Ralph D. Winter and Stephen C. Hawthorne, eds. *Perspectives on the World Christian Movement.* Wm. Carey
    Library.
C. Peter Wagner, *On the Crest of the Wave.* Regal Books.

Discipleship
The 2:7 Series. Navigators, P.O. Box 6000, Colorado
    Springs, CO 80934
Growing by Discipling. Churches Alive, P.O. Box 3800, San
    Bernardino, CA 92413. 714-886-5361.
A Disciple's Bifocals series. ACMC.

These are educational materials about world missions and discipleship materials for your missions planning group.

Mobilization of the Church

Cultivating A Missions-Active Church. ACMC
Stepping Out: A Guide to Short-Term Missions. SMS
    Publication
How Missions-Minded Is Your Church? ACMC
Church Missions Policy Handbook. ACMC
Self-Evaluation Profile. ACMC

Resources for evaluating and mobilizing your local congregation.

*Materials for equipping
and training missions
candidates and
recruits.*

Equipping and Training

Mission Recruits

Lucas and Andry, *Resources for Mission Recruits.* College
Press.

You Can So Get There from Here. MARC/World Vision.

J. Herbert Kane, *The Making of a Missionary.* Baker.

Preparation Workbook for Mission Candidates & Recruits.
Clovernook Christian Church, 1373 W. Galbraith Rd.
Cincinnati, OH 45231

Cross-Cultural Ministry

Lingenfelter and Mayers, *Ministering Cross-Culturally.* Baker.

L. Robert Kohls, *Survival Kit for Overseas Living.* Intercultural
Press.

Paul G. Hiebert, *Anthropological Insights for Missionaries.*
Baker.

*Creative opportunities
for service.*

Non-Traditional Missionaries

Tetsunao Yamamori, *God's New Envoys.* Multnomah.

J. Christy Wilson, Jr. *Today's Tentmakers.* Tyndale.

Lawson Lau, *The World at Your Doorstep.* InterVarsity Press.

K.P. Yohannan, *The Coming Revolution in World Missions.*
Creation House.

Global Opportunities
1600 Elizabeth St., Pasadena, CA 91104
(818) 797-3233
Tentmaking opportunities.

International Students, Inc.
P.O. Box C, Colorado Springs, CO 80901
Resources for international student ministry.

Prayer

Wesley L. Duewel, *Touch the World Through Prayer.*
    Zondervan.
Patrick J. Johnstone, *Operation World.* Multnomah.
Larry Lea, *Could You Not Tarry One Hour?* Creation House.

David Bryant, Concerts of Prayer. InterVarsity Missions.

Global Prayer Digest. Lausanne Committee for World
    Evangelization, Pasadena, CA (818) 798-0819

Change the World School of Prayer
P.O. Box 5838, Mission Hills, CA 91345

✧

*Books and organiza-
tions that will help with
missions prayer
support.*

✧